COVER

THE "GREEN VIOLINIST" IS ONE OF CHAGALL'S PAINTED MEMORIES OF HIS UNCLE, WHO FIDDLED, AND OF HIS BIRTHPLACE IN VITEBSK, RUSSIA.

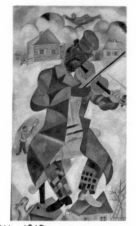

OIL, 1918
SOLOMON R. GUGGENHEIM MUSEUM, N.Y.

THE FIDDLER, THE VIOLIN, THE VIOLET CLOTHES, AND THE SOARING DANCER CREATE A SENSE OF MUSIC THROUGH THE ARTIST'S USE OF COLOR. THE GREEN FACE AND HAND MAKE THE OLD TUNE SEEM NEW AS A FRESH GREEN SPRING. WHILE THE DARK VIOLET COLORS MAY REFLECT THE SADNESS OF THE LONG, HARD, RUSSIAN WINTER, WE ARE WARMED BY THE GLOW FROM THE ORANGE VIOLIN.

Permission ADAGP, 1969, by French Reproduction Rights Inc.

WORLD RIGHTS RESERVED BY ERNEST RABOFF AND GEMINI-SMITH, INC.   FIRST PRINTING 1968

LIBRARY OF CONGRESS CATALOG CARD NO. 68-26549   PRINTED IN JAPAN BY TOPPAN

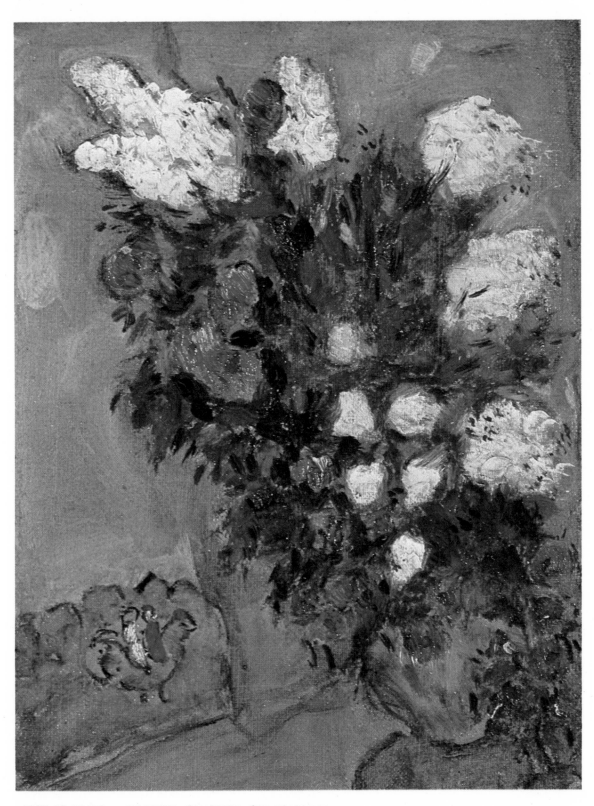

VASE OF LILIES   MAXWELL GALLERIES, SAN FRANCISCO

DEDICATED TO CATHERINE, STEPHEN, DAVID, CHRISTOPHER, DOROTHY AND ROBERT WILLOUGHBY

MARC CHAGALL

By Ernest Raboff

ART FOR CHILDREN

A GEMINI-SMITH BOOK

EDITED BY BRADLEY SMITH

PUBLISHED BY
DOUBLEDAY & CO., INC.

GARDEN CITY, NEW YORK
1968

MARC CHAGALL WAS BORN ON JULY 7, 1887. HIS BIRTHPLACE WAS A SMALL RUSSIAN VILLAGE CALLED VITEBSK.

ZAHAR CHAGALL, HIS FATHER, WORKED IN A HERRING PACKING HOUSE. HIS SON REMEMBERS HIM AS A TALL, QUIET AND SHY MAN WHO WAS ALWAYS WORKING.

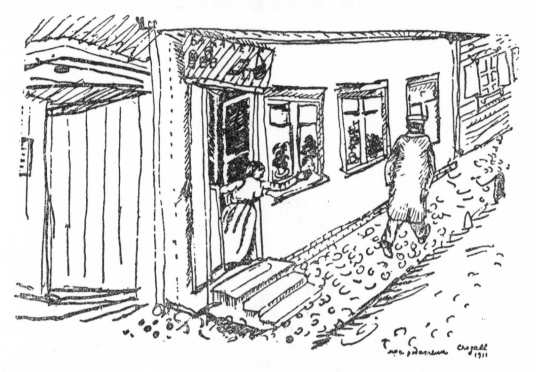

FEIGA-ITA, HIS MOTHER, HAD EIGHT OTHER CHILDREN BESIDES HER OLDEST SON, MARC. SHE HAD A SMALL SHOP IN HER HOME WHERE SHE SOLD HERRING, FLOUR, SUGAR, AND SPICES TO ADD TO THE FAMILY INCOME.

CHAGALL MOVED TO FRANCE IN 1923. FROM 1941 UNTIL 1948, HE LIVED IN THE UNITED STATES. THEN HE RETURNED TO FRANCE, BUT IT WAS THE MEMORIES OF RUSSIA THAT HE PAINTED AND FOR WHICH HE IS MOST FAMOUS.

MARC CHAGALL SAID: "TO KEEP THE EARTH ON ONE'S ROOTS AND FIND ANOTHER EARTH...THAT IS A REAL MIRACLE."

ON **PAINTING** AS A MEANS OF SELF-EXPRESSION: "IT WAS MORE NECESSARY FOR ME THAN FOOD. IT SEEMED TO ME LIKE A WINDOW THROUGH WHICH I COULD HAVE TAKEN FLIGHT TOWARD ANOTHER WORLD."

"AS I GROW OLDER I SEE MORE CLEARLY AND DISTINCTLY WHAT IS RIGHT AND WRONG IN OUR WAY OF LIFE AND HOW RIDICULOUS IS EVERYTHING NOT ACHIEVED WITH ONE'S OWN BLOOD AND ONE'S OWN SOUL, EVERYTHING NOT INFUSED WITH LOVE."

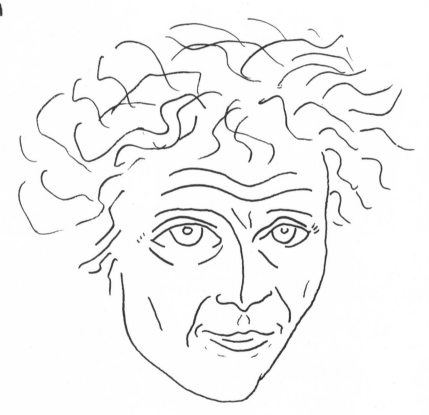

"EVERYTHING CAN AND WILL BE TRANSFORMED IN LIFE AND IN ART, IF WE SPEAK THE WORD LOVE WITHOUT SHAME... IN IT LIES TRUE ART..."

PORTRAIT OF THE ARTIST BY RABOFF

"MIDSUMMER NIGHT'S DREAM" IS A PLAY BY WILLIAM SHAKESPEARE IN WHICH A MAN IN LOVE IS TURNED INTO A DONKEY. CHAGALL HAS PAINTED THIS IDEA SHOWING, IN HIS OWN WAY, HOW THE MAN IS CHANGED. EACH OF US CAN ENJOY FINDING THE MEANING FOR OURSELVES IN THIS PAINTING.

ONE FIRST NOTICES THE ANIMAL HEAD ON THE MAN'S BODY, THEN THE DREAM-LIKE FACE OF THE BRIDE. THE RED ANGEL SEEMS TO BE FLYING TOWARD THE HORNS OF THE ANIMAL HEAD. NOTICE HOW THE GLOWING LIGHT OF THE ANGEL BRIGHTLY SHOWS ON THE FLOWERING TREE AND ON THE GREEN FIDDLING CLOWN.

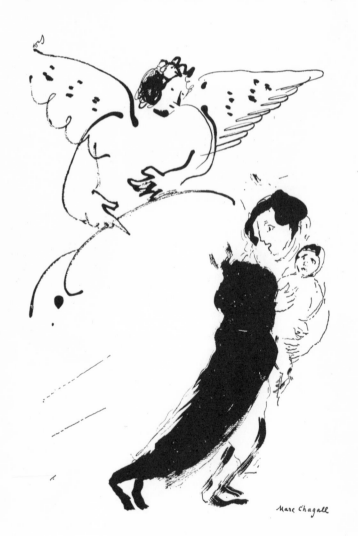

Marc Chagall

CHAGALL MAY BE SAYING THAT MAN, EVEN THOUGH AN ANIMAL, HAS THE ABILITY WITHIN HIM TO BE A CLOWN, A LOVER AND A MUSICIAN.

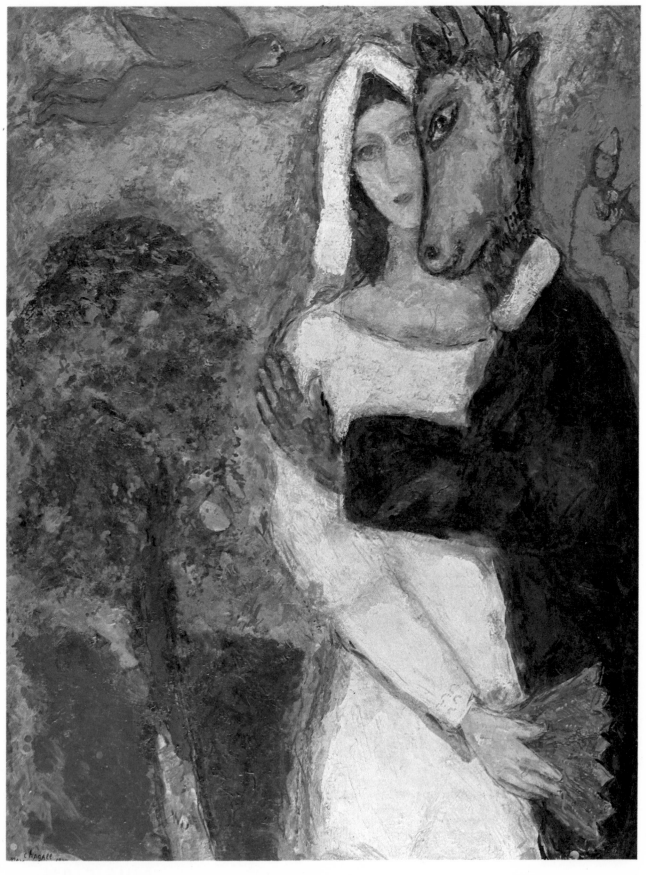

MIDSUMMER NIGHT'S DREAM   1939   MUSEUM OF PAINTING AND SCULPTURE , GRENOBLE , FRANCE

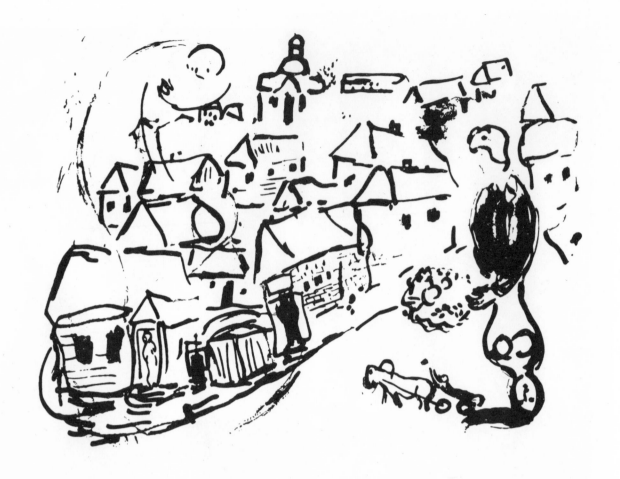

"THE THREE CANDLES" IS A DRAMATIC AND POWERFUL COMPOSITION. THE CANDLES, THE BRIDE AND GROOM, THE WOMEN WITH RAISED ARMS BEHIND A POINTED PICKET FENCE, THE HARLEQUIN STANDING ON A STOOL——ALL POINT UPWARDS LIKE ROCKETS TOWARDS THE SKY. AS THOUGH EXPLODING, THEY SHOWER THE EARTH WITH FLOWERS AND GREEN LEAVES, TUMBLING ANGELS, AND WITH THE HAPPY VIOLINIST CHAGALL OFTEN PAINTED.

THE BRIDEGROOM, HOLDING HIS WIFE IN HIS ARMS, LOOKS STARTLED AND AMAZED. THE HOUSES ARE VERY STILL, AND EVEN THE ANIMAL RESTS CONTENTEDLY UNDER THE CANDLES.

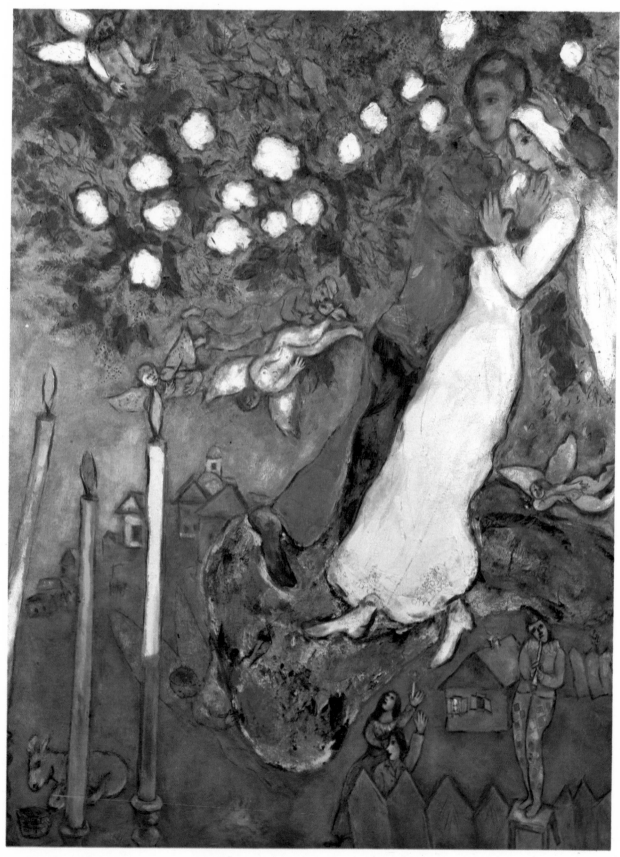

THREE CANDLES   READER'S DIGEST COLLECTION, PLEASANTVILLE, NEW YORK

"I AND THE VILLAGE" IS AS MUCH FUN AS IT IS BEAUTIFUL.

THE EYE OF THE COW, CENTERED IN THE PICTURE, SEES MANY THINGS. WITHIN ITS HEAD IS THE VISION OF ITSELF WITH THE MILKMAID. OUTSIDE ITSELF IT IS AWARE OF A PERSON FACING IT, PERHAPS THE ARTIST.

IN THE LOWER LEFT CORNER THE SUN AND MOON ARE COMBINED AND REPEAT A PATTERN THAT MAKES A DIAGONAL PATH ACROSS THE PICTURE.

IN THE UPPER RIGHT SIDE A PRIEST STANDS IN THE DOORWAY OF HIS CHURCH.

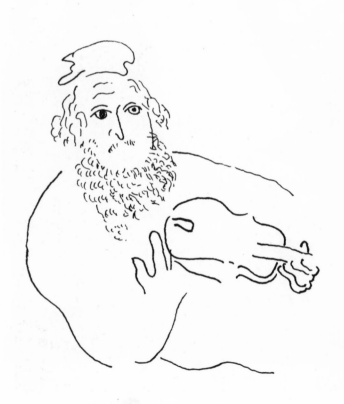

CHAGALL SHOWS US THE VILLAGE FROM MANY POINTS OF VIEW, RIGHT SIDE UP AND UPSIDE DOWN. THE HAPPINESS OF THE ARTIST AND OF THE LIFE OF THE VILLAGE IS SHOWN BY THE COLORFUL BEADS WORN BY THE COW AND THE SMILE ON THE LIPS OF THE PERSON ON THE RIGHT.

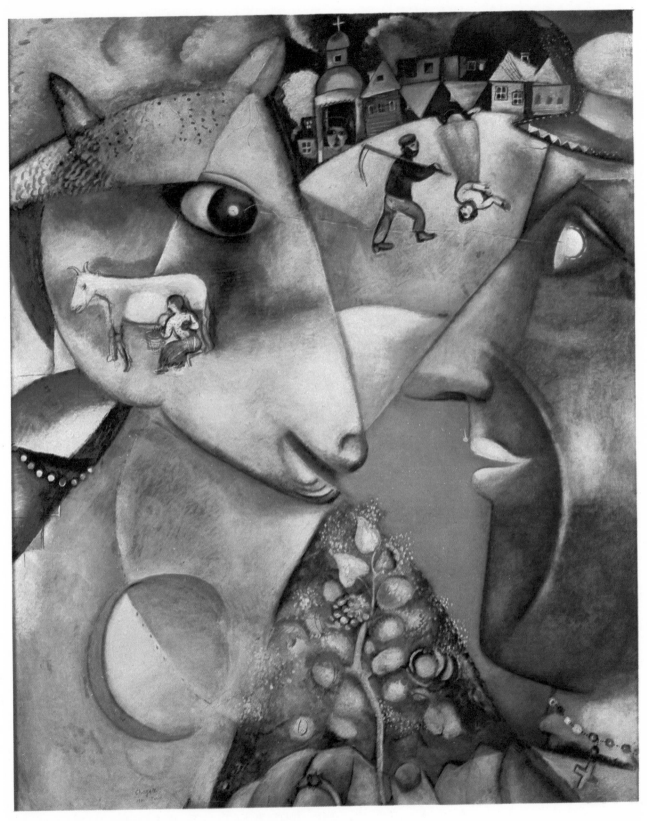

I AND THE VILLAGE   1911   THE MUSEUM OF MODERN ART, NEW YORK

CHAGALL'S PAINTING OF "THE POET" IS LIKE A POEM WRITTEN WITH PICTURES INSTEAD OF WORDS.

THE POSITION OF THE POET'S HEAD IMMEDIATELY ATTRACTS OUR ATTENTION. LIKE POETS AND PAINTERS, EVERYONE DAYDREAMS AT TIMES. DO YOU EVER FEEL AS IF YOUR HEAD AND MIND COULD FLOAT, TWIST, AND TURN BACKWARDS, SIDEWAYS, OR UPSIDE DOWN? OUR IMAGINATIONS CAN ALMOST CARRY US AWAY FROM OUR BODIES.

ARTISTS OFTEN TRAIN THEIR MINDS SO THAT THEY CAN LOSE THEMSELVES IN THOUGHT WHEREVER THEY ARE WORKING. IT IS PART OF THEIR PROFESSION TO SHARE WITH US THE RESULTS OF THESE IMAGININGS.

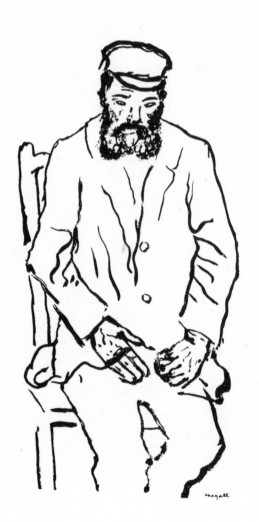

THIS POET SEEMS LOST IN THOUGHT AS HE SITS WITH HIS PEN, A CIGARETTE, AND HIS AFFECTIONATE CAT. THE FLOWERS OF HIS THINKING FLOAT NEARBY. THE BLUE SKY IS REPEATED IN THE BOTTLE AND HIS CLOTHES. LIKE THE FACETS OF A DIAMOND, EACH ANGLE HAS A BEAUTY OF ITS OWN.

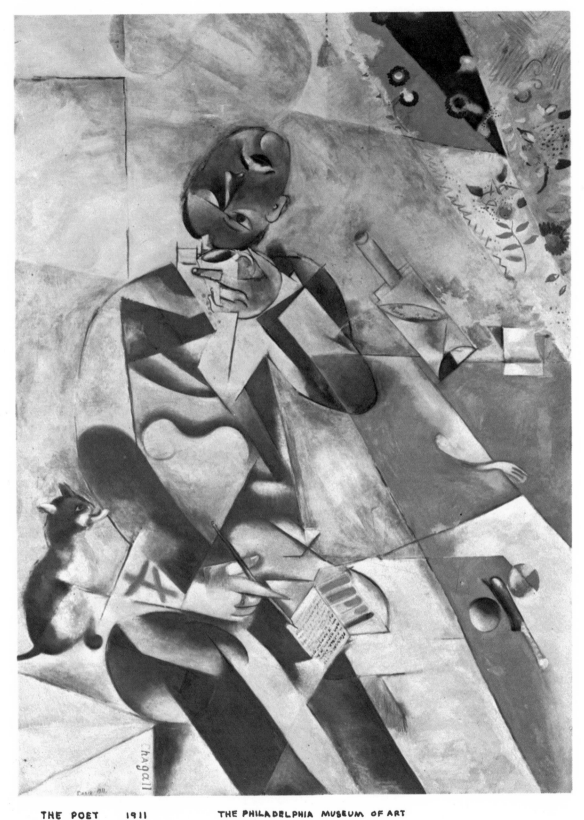

THE POET   1911   THE PHILADELPHIA MUSEUM OF ART

IN "THREE ACROBATS" CHAGALL USES FORM WITH
COLOR, AND VERY LITTLE LINE TO TELL THE STORY.
THE PERFORMING WOMAN IS THE STAR OF THE ACT.

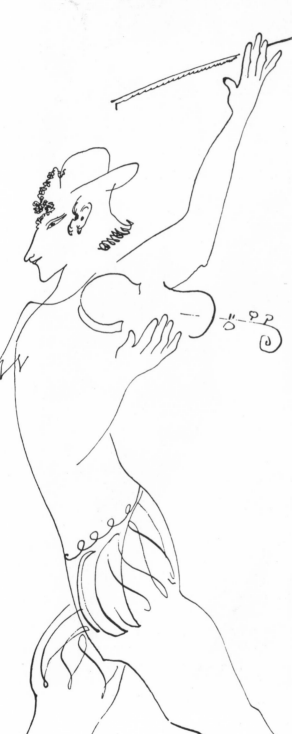

HER HEAD, FRAMED
BY HER ARM AND
RAISED LEG,
ATTRACTS US FIRST.
THEN OUR EYES MOVE
TO THE OUTSTRETCHED
ARM, DOWN THE
BLUE CURTAIN, AND
TO THE WAITING
ACROBAT IN THE
RED SHIRT. HIS FEET POINT
US ACROSS THE BRIGHT
CARPET TO THE BOUQUET OF
FLOWERS, THEN UP THE RIGHT
SIDE OF THE PICTURE. HERE,
THE THIRD ACROBAT, WITH ARM
ON HEAD, GUIDES US UP THE
OTHER BLUE DECORATED CURTAIN
TO COMPLETE THE TRIANGULAR
PATTERN.

THE WOMAN'S TWO ASSISTANTS,
PERHAPS LIKE US, GAZE IN WONDER
AT HER FINE PERFORMANCE.

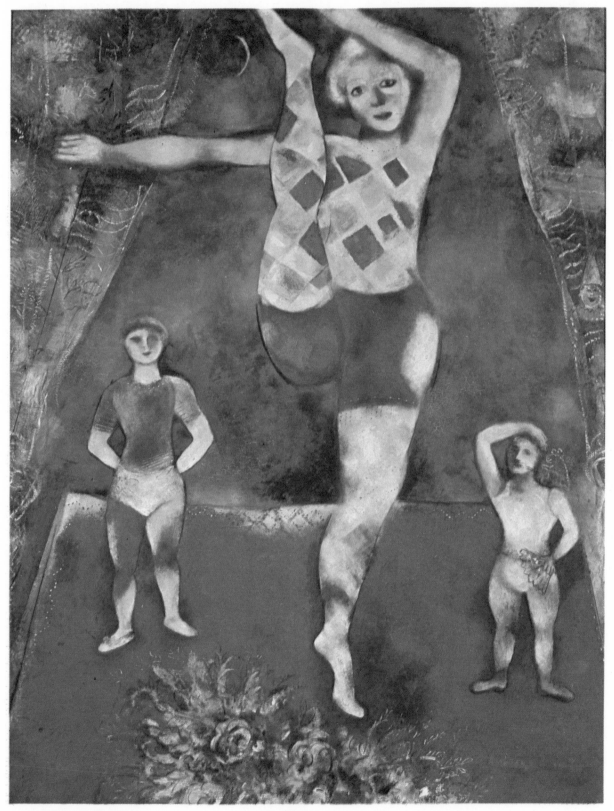

THREE ACROBATS   OIL   S.F. BRODY COLLECTION, LOS ANGELES

"VASE OF FLOWERS" GLOWS LIKE AN OUTDOOR FIRE IN THE BLUE OF THE NIGHT SKY. THE BOUQUET FILLS THE NIGHT WITH COLOR AND FRAGRANCE.

THE SOUNDS OF THE EVENING ARE REPRESENTED BY THE VIOLINIST IN THE UPPER LEFT CORNER.

THE ANIMAL ON THE ROOF SEEMS TO BE A SYMBOL OF SECURITY AND PEACE.

THE MOON IS REFLECTED IN A HALO OF LIGHT AROUND THE RESTING ANIMAL'S HEAD.

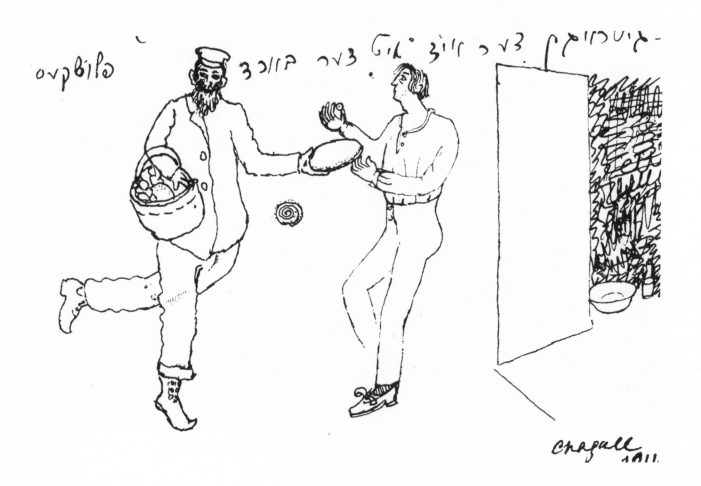

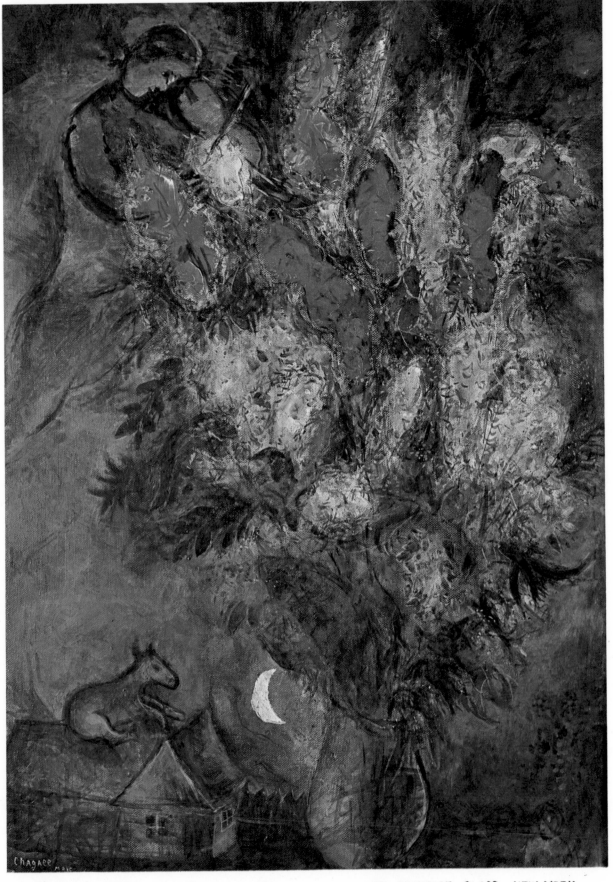

VASE OF FLOWERS, BY MOONLIGHT 1943   MRS. BEATRICE GLASS, NEW YORK

"PARIS THROUGH A WINDOW" IS A COLORFUL AND EXCITING PAINTING. CHAGALL ENJOYED DRAWING SCENES OF PARIS AND ITS LANDMARKS SUCH AS THE EIFFEL TOWER. HE NEVER TIRED OF LOOKING AT AND PAINTING THIS QUEEN OF CITIES.

THE TWO LOVERS WALK CLOSE TOGETHER AND THE ARTIST HAS PAINTED THEM HEAD TO HEAD. THE UPSIDE DOWN TRAIN IS PART OF CHAGALL'S PARIS SCENE. IT PUFFS A COLUMN OF SMOKE LIKE A SIGNATURE ACROSS THE STREETS.

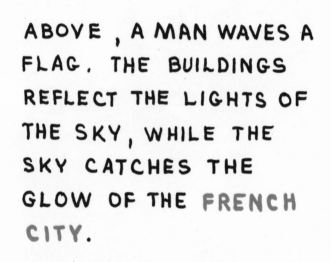

ABOVE , A MAN WAVES A FLAG. THE BUILDINGS REFLECT THE LIGHTS OF THE SKY, WHILE THE SKY CATCHES THE GLOW OF THE FRENCH CITY.

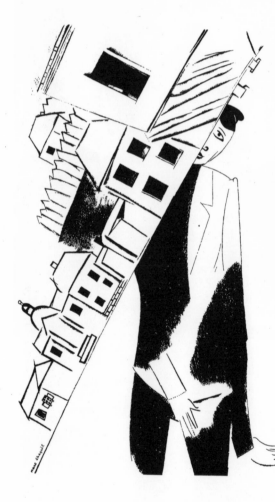

THE WINDOW FRAME MIRRORS THE MANY COLORS SEEN OUTSIDE.

THE CAT, PAINTED WITH HUMAN FEATURES, IS A GOOD FRIEND AND COMPANION.

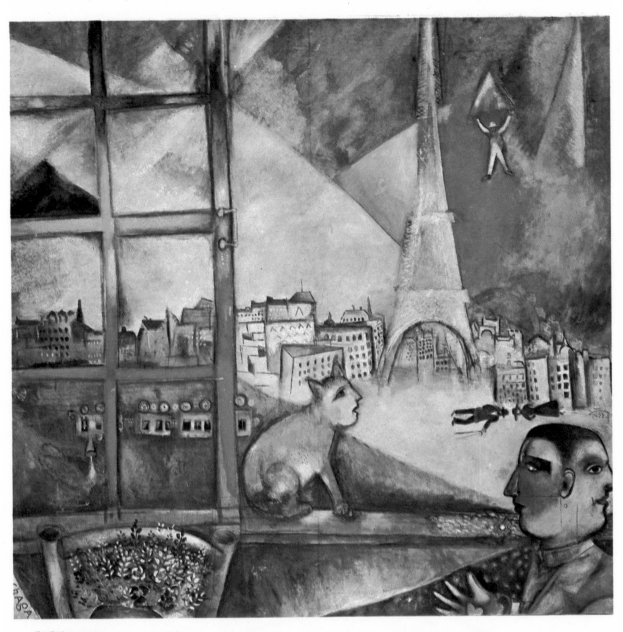

PARIS THROUGH A WINDOW   SOLOMON R. GUGGENHEIM MUSEUM, NEW YORK

CHAGALL SHOWS US IN "THE ACROBAT" HOW UNUSUALLY LONG THE ARMS, BODIES, AND LEGS OF THESE ENTERTAINERS APPEAR TO BE AS THEY PERFORM THEIR AMAZING FEATS.

IN THE FRENCH CIRCUSES, THE ACROBATS DRESS IN COSTUMES OF CLOWNS OR HARLEQUINS. THEY RESEMBLE PINWHEELS OF FLASHING COLORS AS THEY DIVE THROUGH HOOPS, DO BACKFLIPS, AND A SERIES OF SOMERSAULTS.

THE ARTIST MAKES ACROBATS OF OUR EYES ALSO. OUR ATTENTION MOVES IN CIRCLES AS WE LOOK FROM THE HEAD TO THE RUFFLED COLLAR, THE ARMS, THE HOOP, COSTUME, AND FINALLY TO THE RUNNING LEGS.

EVEN THE DESIGNS AND PATTERNS OF THE COSTUME EXPRESS A FEELING OF ACTION AND MOVEMENT.

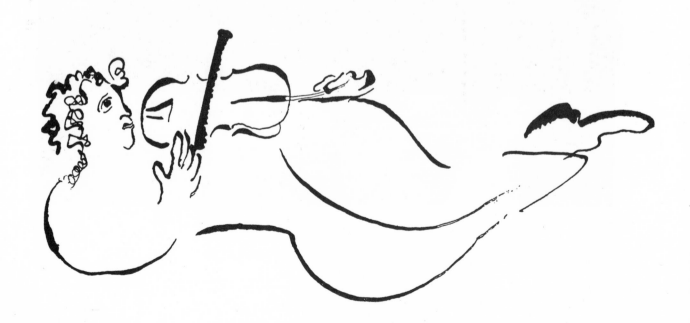

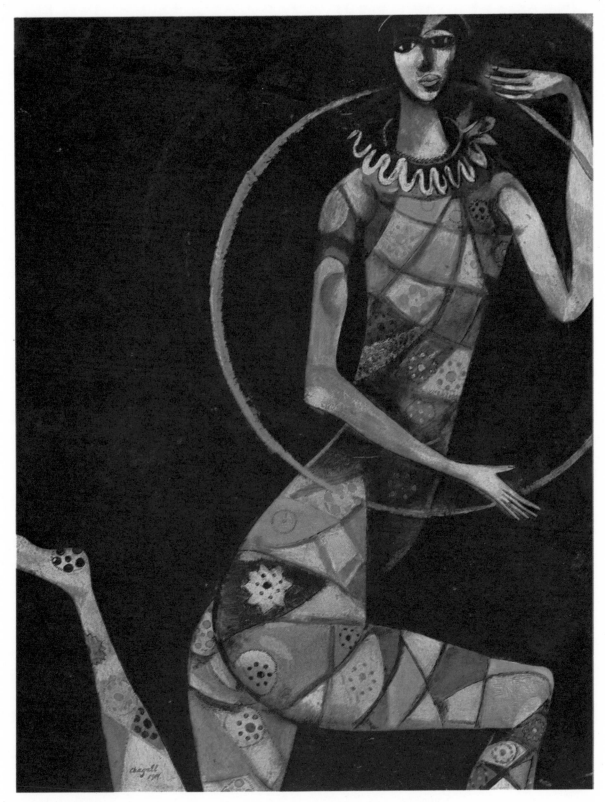

THE ACROBAT   1914   ALBRIGHT-KNOX ART GALLERY , BUFFALO

"PEASANT LIFE" IS THE STORY OF A SMALL VILLAGE TOLD FOR US IN PAINT BY A GREAT STORYTELLER. CHAGALL SHOWS THE PLEASANT EVERYDAY LIFE OF THE VILLAGE'S RURAL PEOPLE.

NOTICE THE FARMER'S WELL-FED HORSE. THIS IS THE PEASANT'S MOST IMPORTANT FELLOW WORKER AS WELL AS HIS LOVED COMPANION.

THE COTTAGE, WITH ITS WINDOWS AND SHUTTERS, THE GAS LANTERN, AND THE TREE FORM THE SETTING FOR THIS PICTURE-STORY. THE HORSE AND CART ARE READY TO TAKE THE VILLAGE FAMILY WITH THEIR MANY FARM PRODUCTS TO MARKET.

THE DANCING COUPLE COMPLETES CHAGALL'S COLORFUL PICTURE OF PEASANT LIFE.

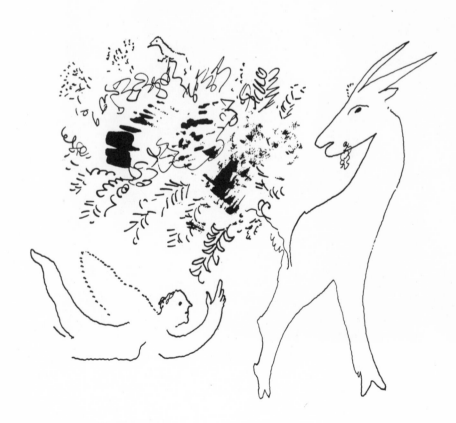

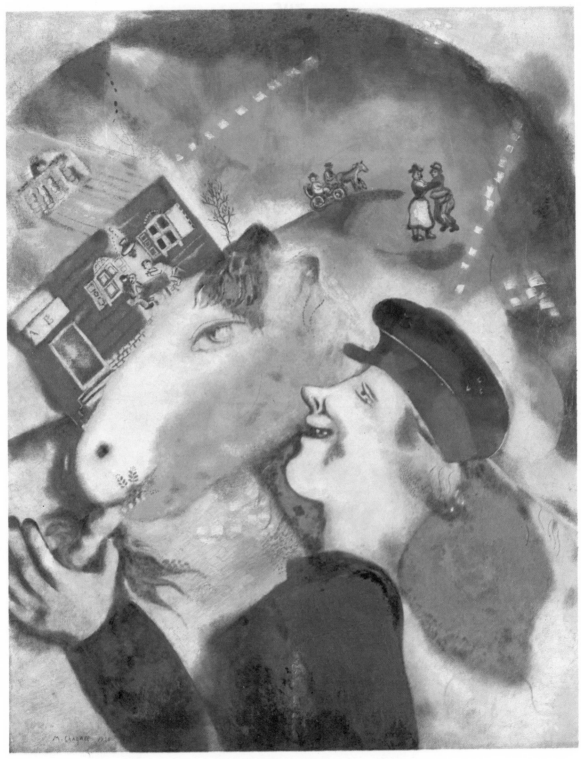

PEASANT LIFE   ALBRIGHT - KNOX ART GALLERY , BUFFALO

IN "THE BIRTHDAY" CHAGALL SHOWS US HOW HE FELT ON ONE OF HIS BIRTHDAYS. IN THE PICTURE, AS IN HIS MEMORY, HE FLOATS INTO THE HOME OF BELLA, HIS FUTURE BRIDE. SHE GREETS HIM WITH A BOUQUET OF FLOWERS AND A KISS.

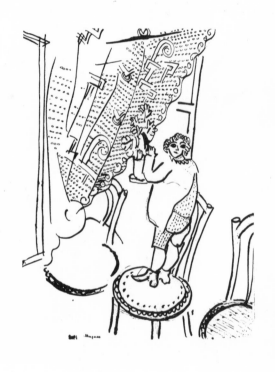

HER DRESS AND ONE FOOT ARE CAUGHT UP IN THE BREEZE OF THE ARTIST'S MOTION.

HER PURSE LIES ON THE TABLE IN FRONT OF THE CAKE SHE HAS BAKED. BESIDE IT IS A GLASS FOR WINE AND A PIECE OF WATERMELON.

THE BRIGHT RED OF THE FLOOR, THE TABLE, AND THE BEDSPREAD ADDS A WARM GLOW TO THE ROOM.

THROUGH THE WINDOW WE CAN SEE THE QUIET STREET, THE NEIGHBOR'S PICKET FENCE AND THE STARS IN THE EVENING SKY.

CHAGALL HAS PAINTED HIS JOYOUS BIRTHDAY MEMORY FOR EVERYONE TO SHARE.

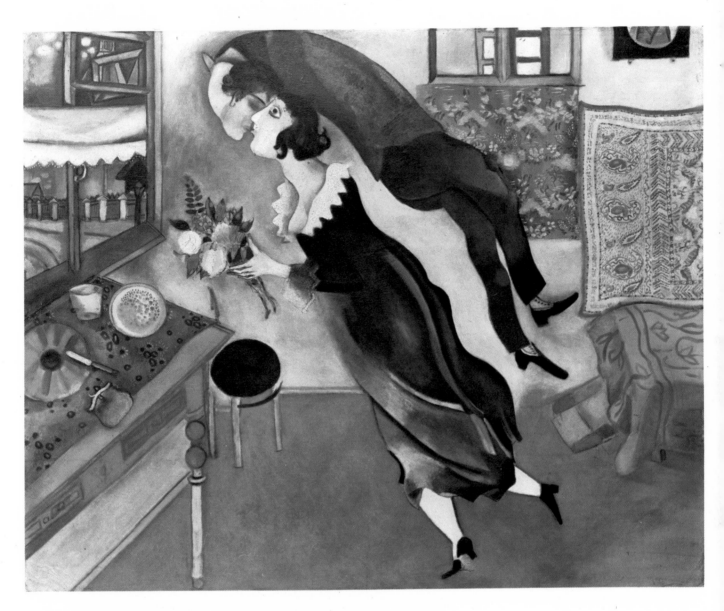

THE   BIRTHDAY , 1915   THE MUSEUM OF MODERN ART , NEW YORK

ONE SHOULD STUDY "TIME IS A RIVER WITHOUT BANKS"
TO EXPLORE THE FULL MEANING OF THE TITLE.

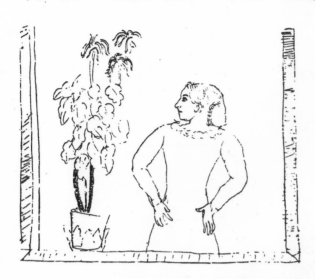

THE CURIOUS FLYING
FISH PLAYING THE
VIOLIN REFLECTS THE
COLOR AND FLAMES OF
THE SUN ON ITS WINGS
AND MOUTH.

ON ONE BANK OF THE
RIVER A YOUNG COUPLE
IS UNAWARE OF GRANDFATHER TIME TICKING AWAY
THE HOURS. THEY HEAR ONLY THE MUSIC.

ON THE OTHER SIDE, CURVING AROUND THE HORIZON
ARE THE HOUSES OF THE CITY. THEY STAND SILENTLY,
HOLDING THE HISTORY OF TIME AND THE RIVER
IN THEIR WORN BRICKS AND STONE WALLS.

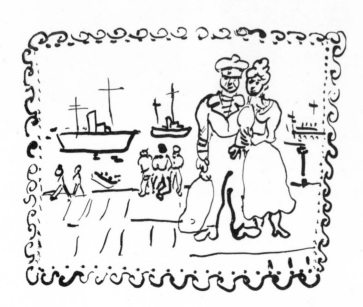

THE BLUE OF THE
DAY AND THE DARKER
BLUE OF NIGHT
FILL THE CANVAS
WITH COLOR.

A LONE FISHERMAN
PADDLES HIS WAY
INTO THE FUTURE.

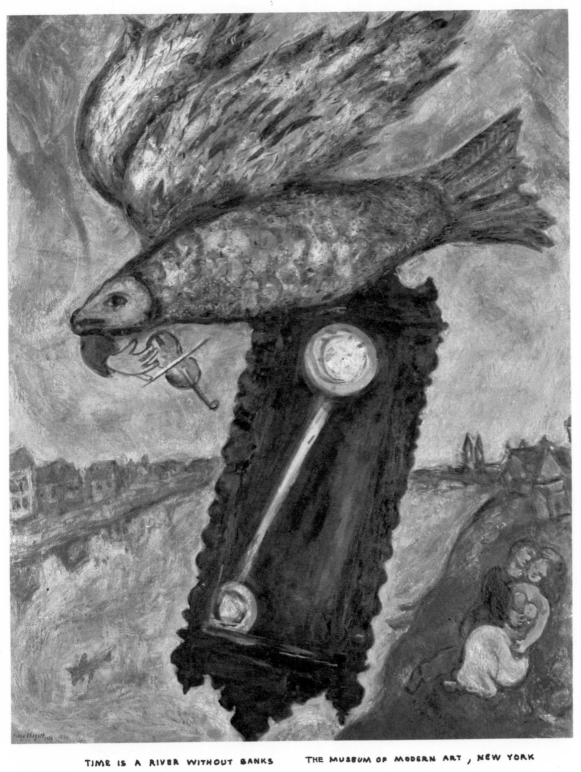

TIME IS A RIVER WITHOUT BANKS   THE MUSEUM OF MODERN ART, NEW YORK

"THE FIDDLER" WHO PLAYS HIS VIOLIN IN MANY OF
CHAGALL'S PAINTINGS WAS IN REALITY A FAVORITE
UNCLE. THE ARTIST KNEW OF THE FAMOUS RUSSIAN STORY
BY SHOLEM ALEICHEM ABOUT A FIDDLER WHO PLAYED FROM
THE ROOF TOPS. IN THIS PICTURE, CHAGALL PLACED HIS
FIDDLER WITH ONE FOOT ON THE ROOF. WHEN THE FIDDLER
PLAYED IT WAS AS THOUGH HE WERE DANCING ABOVE THE
ROOFS AND AS IF HIS MUSIC TOOK HIM UP AMONG THE
ANGELS, CLOSE TO HEAVEN.

TO SHOW THAT HE ENJOYED HIS MUSICAL UNCLE WHILE
HE WAS SMALL, WHEN HE WAS GROWING UP, AND WHEN HE

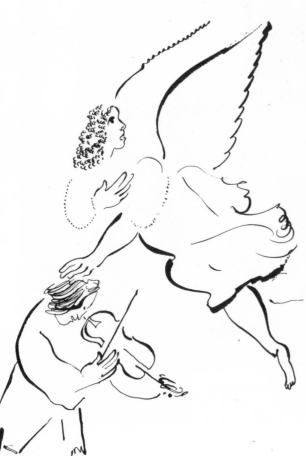

WAS A YOUNG MAN, CHAGALL
PAINTED HIMSELF WITH THREE
HEADS IN THE LOWER LEFT SIDE
OF THE PICTURE.

THE HOUSES ARE ALL LIGHTED
EITHER FROM WITHIN OR FROM
WITHOUT AS THOUGH THE PEOPLE
MIGHT BE LISTENING TO THE
MUSIC IN THE NIGHT.

IN THE LOWER RIGHT CORNER
SOME OF THE BIRDS ALSO
LISTEN WHILE OTHERS SEEM
TO BE SINGING WITH THE
FIDDLER.

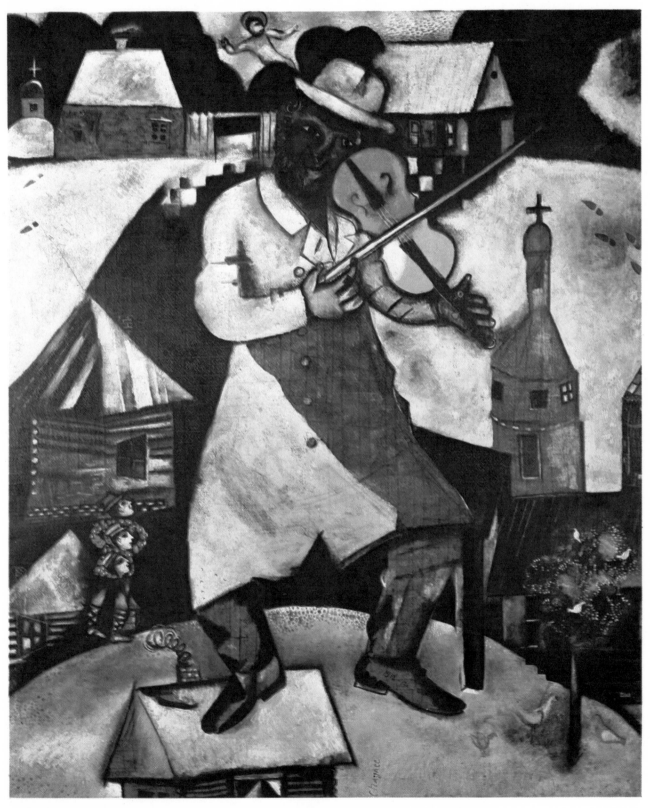

VIOLINIST   OIL, 1912-13   STEDELIJK MUSEUM, AMSTERDAM

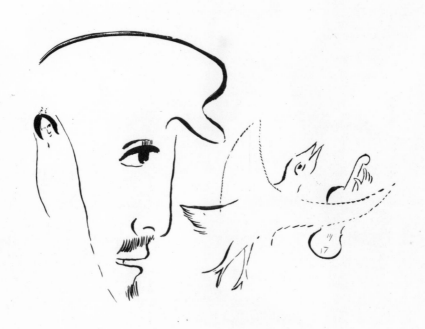